Adult Coloring book Farm Animals

Vol 5

By: L. M. Boelz

I want to take a moment to thank you for purchasing this coloring book.

A lot of time went into the making of it. I wanted to be able to give you hours of fun

and relaxation. So Enjoy. Be sure to check out my other coloring books if you

like this one.   There are 20 different pictures to color in this book.

Other titles

Chickens Vol. 1

Southwest, Floral Vol 2

Day of the Dead & Madri Gras Vol 3

Dragons & Castles Vol 4

pages

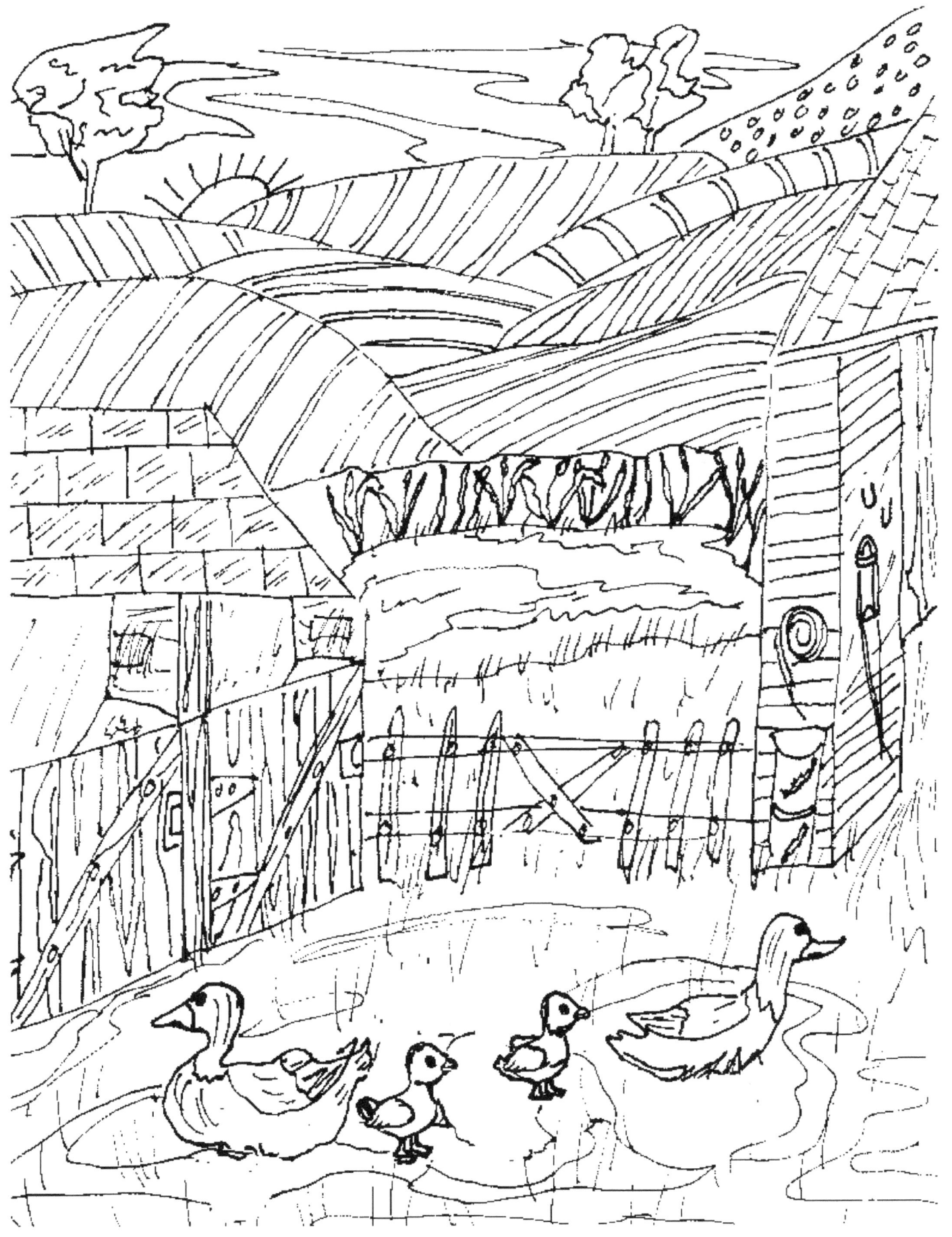

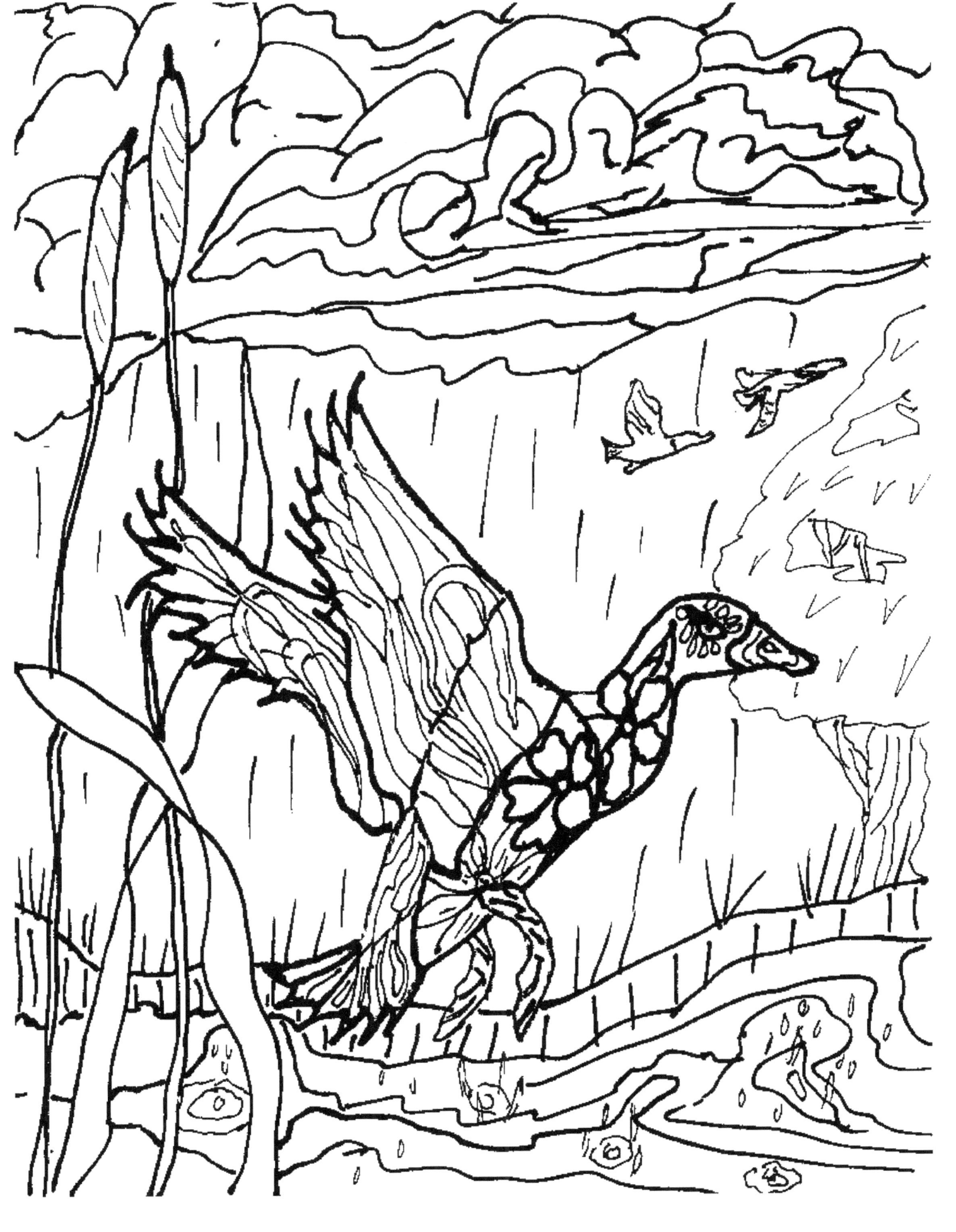

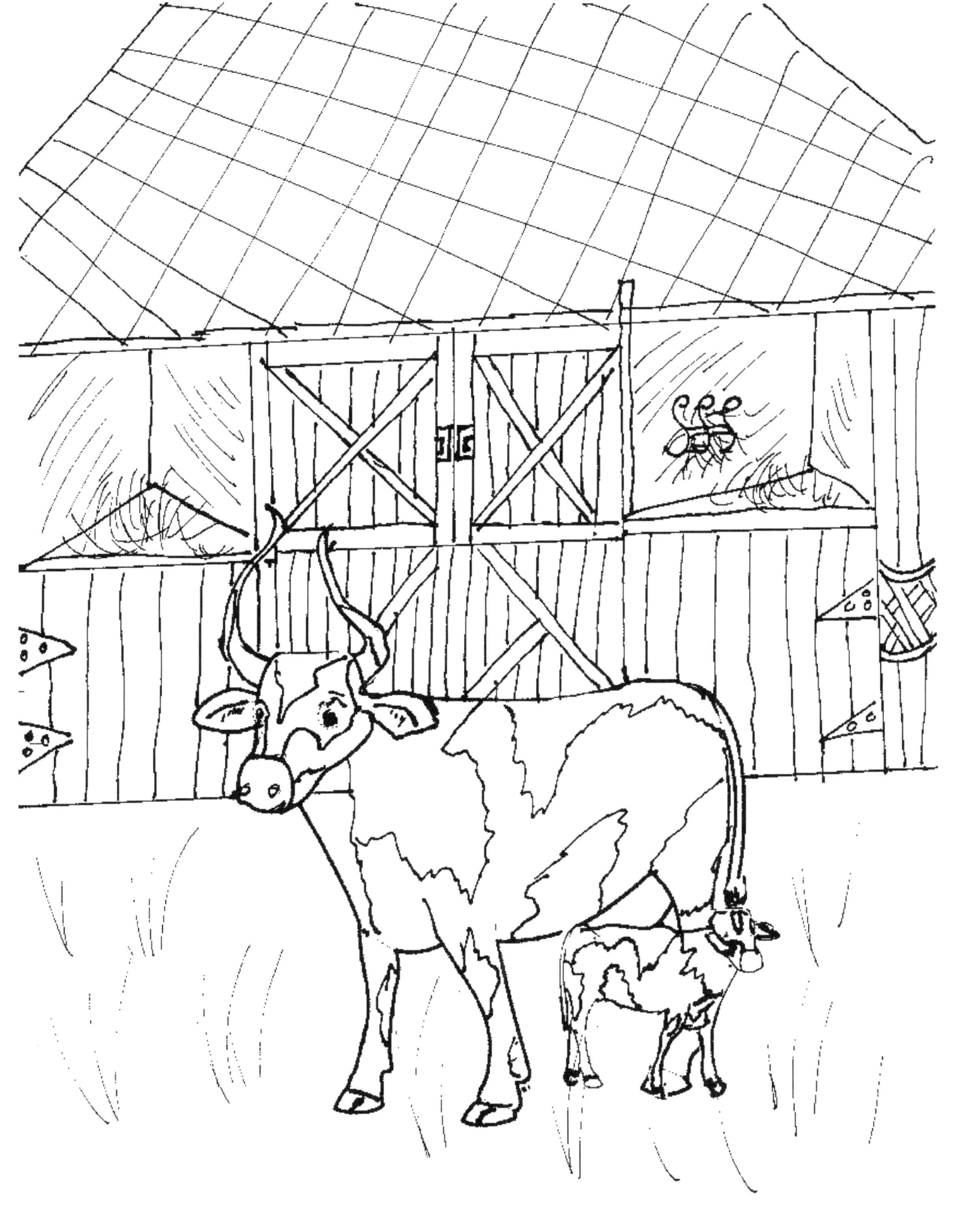

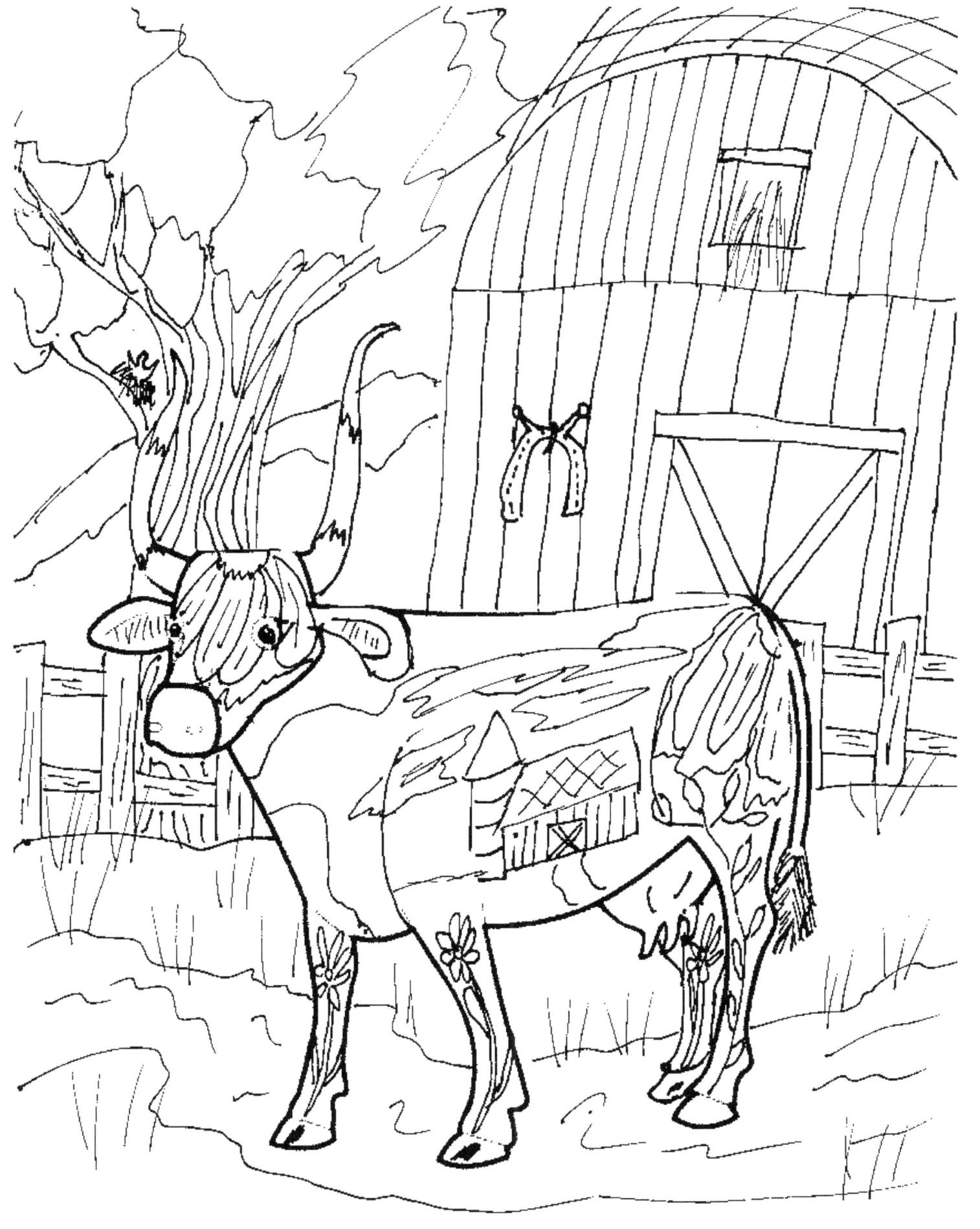

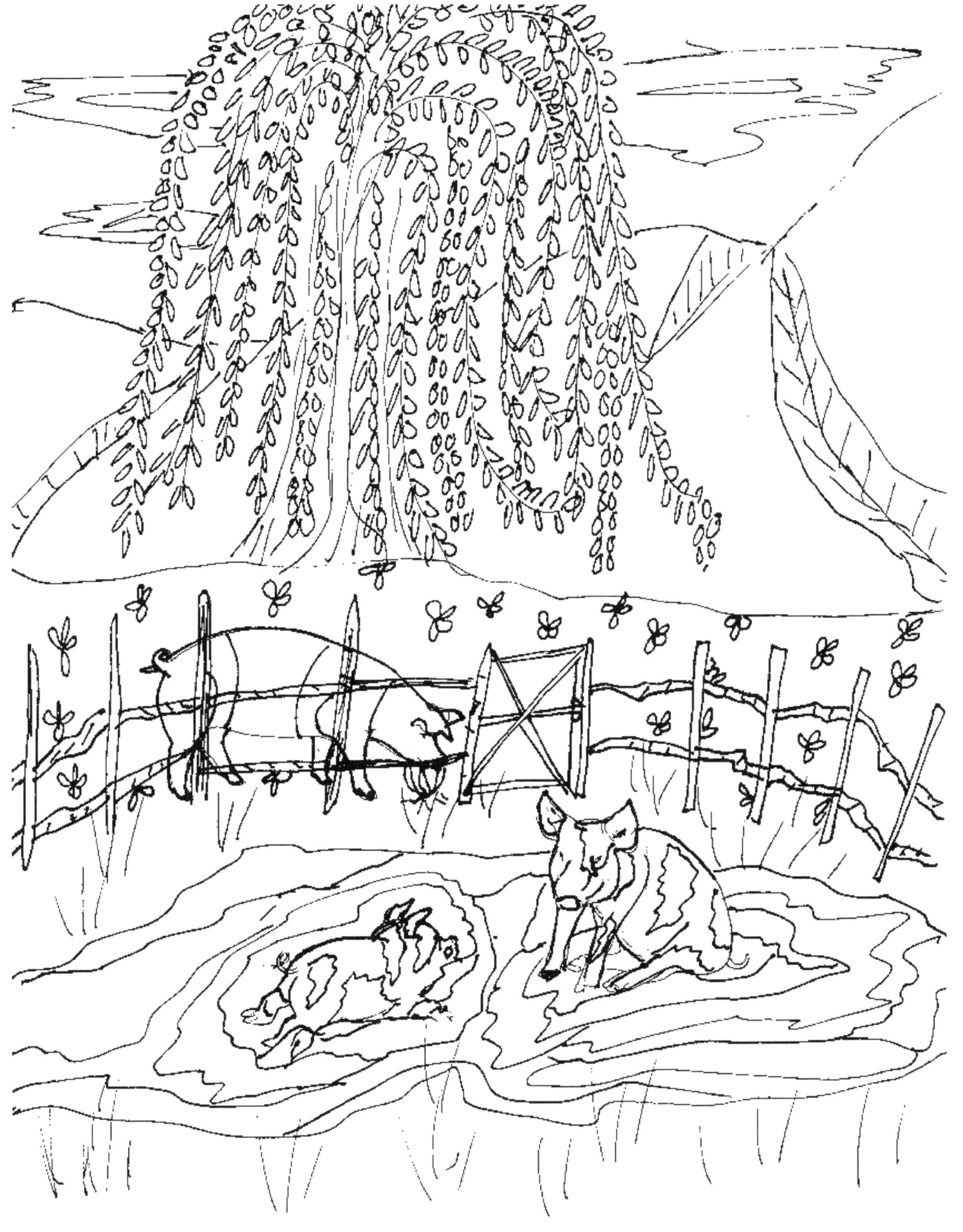

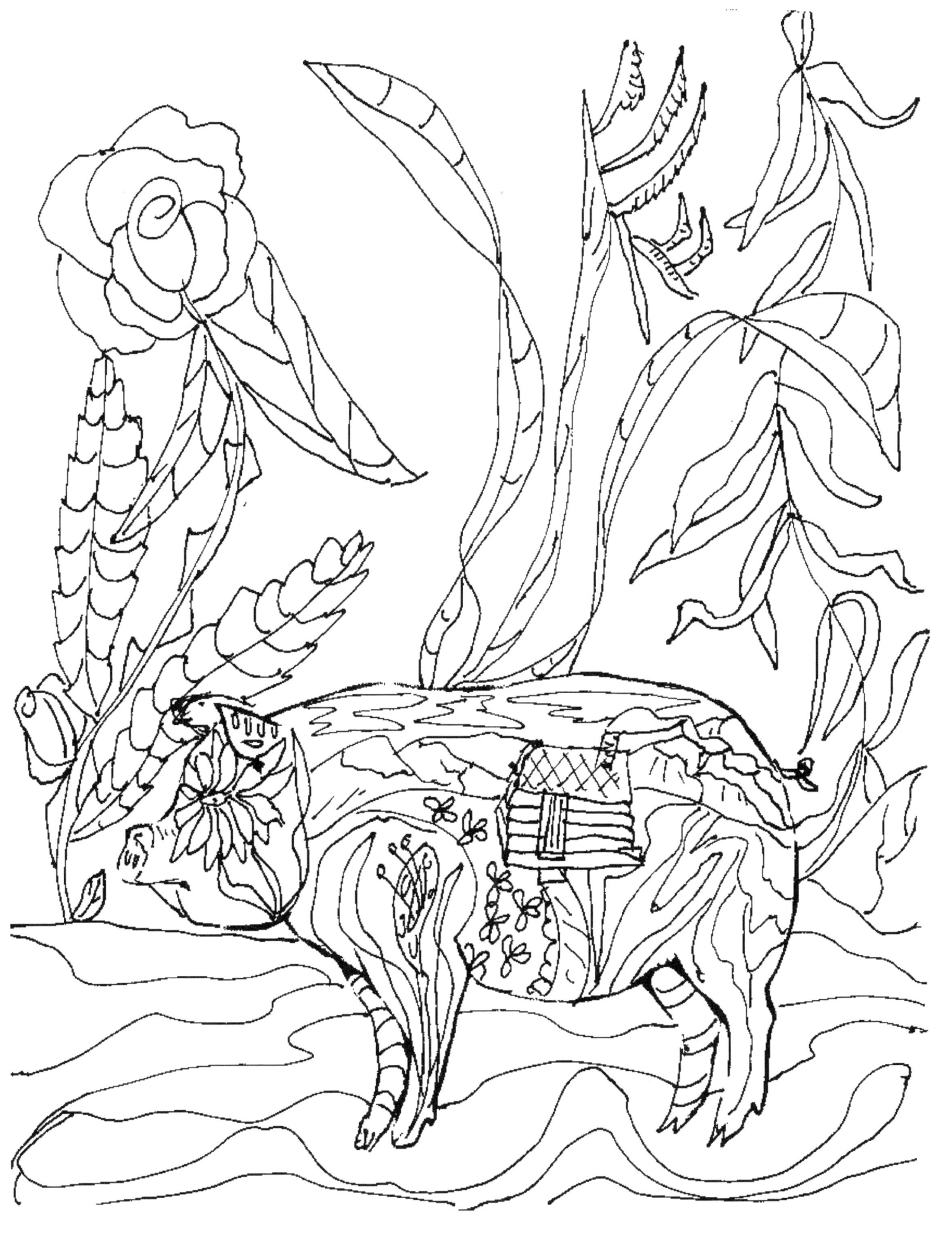

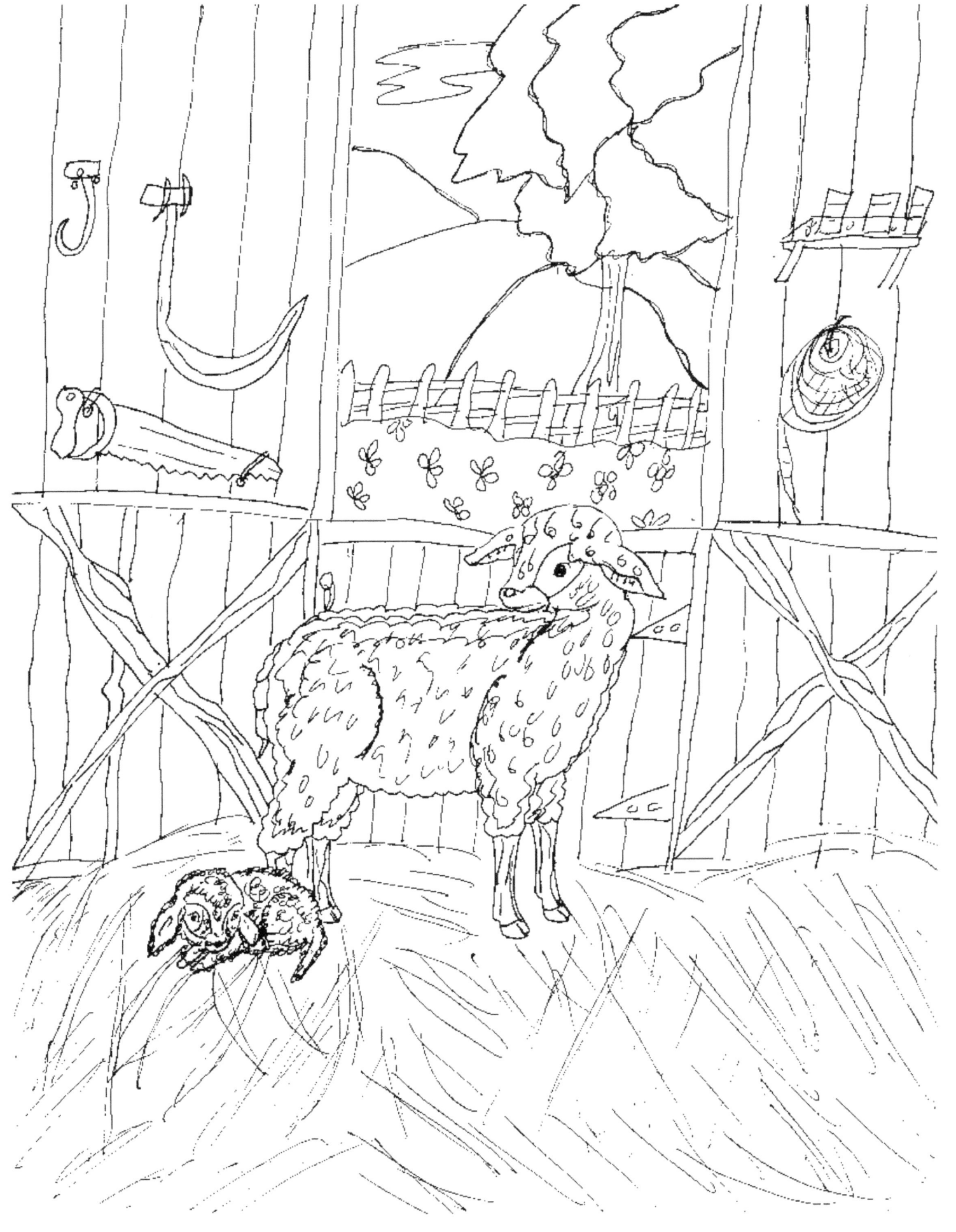

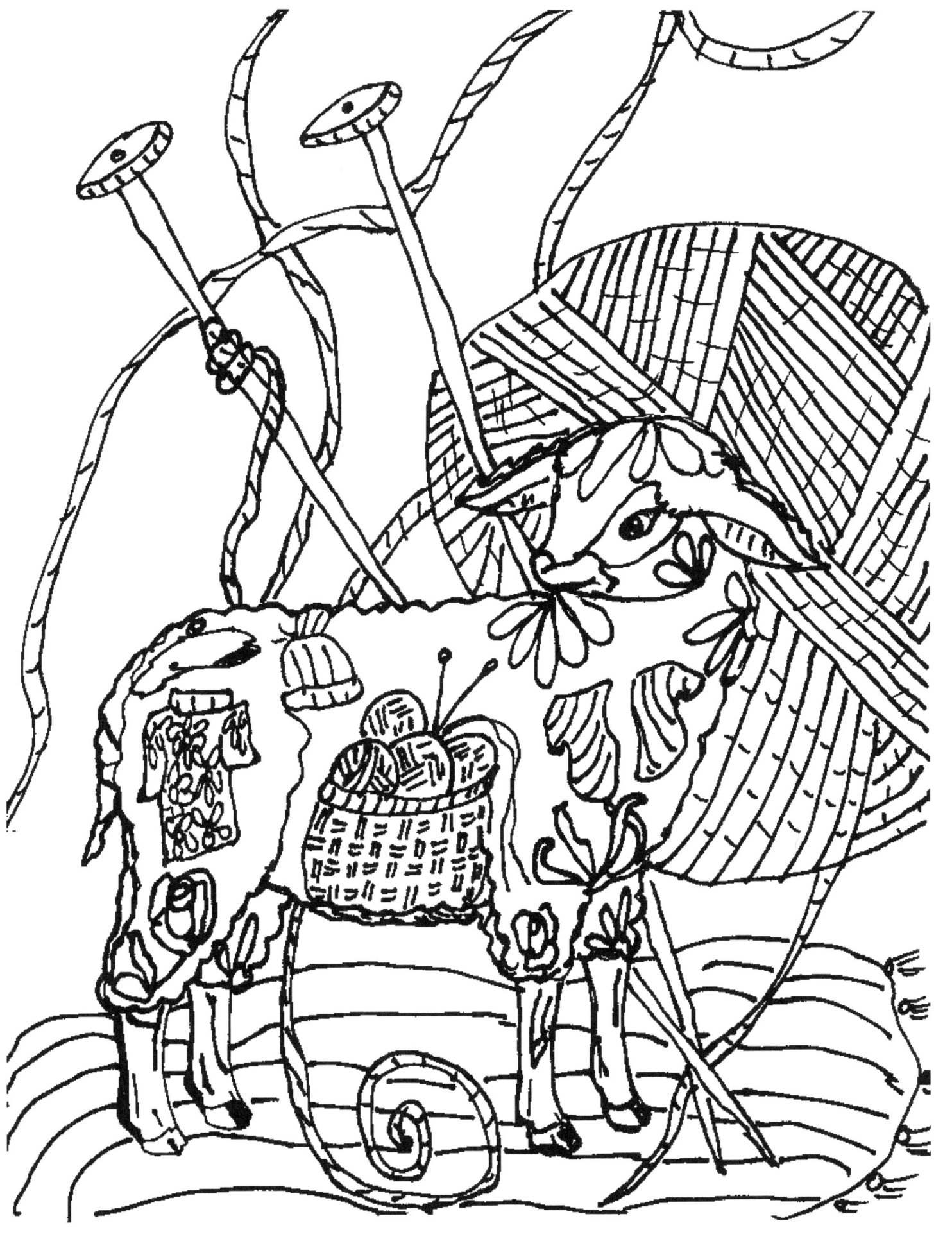

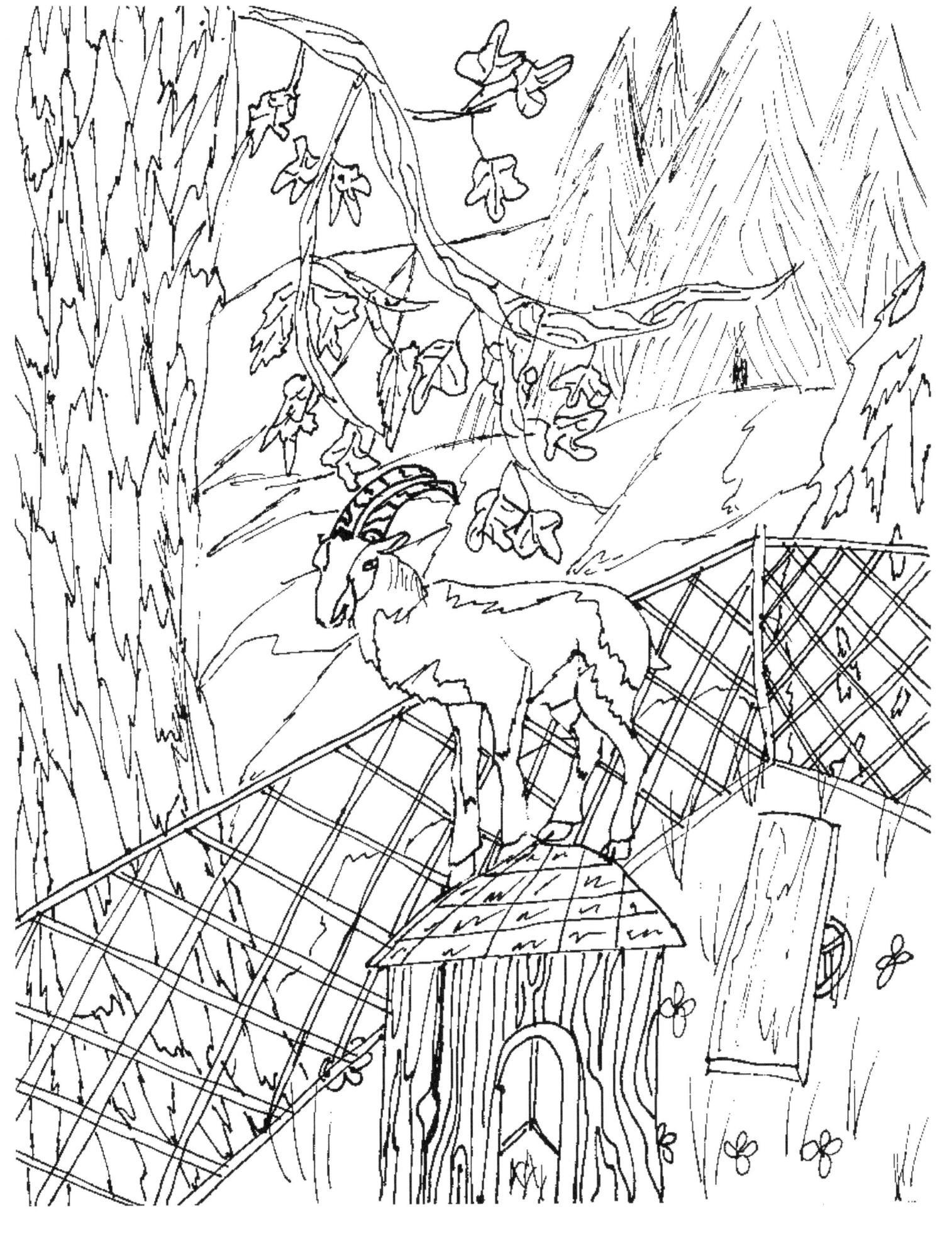

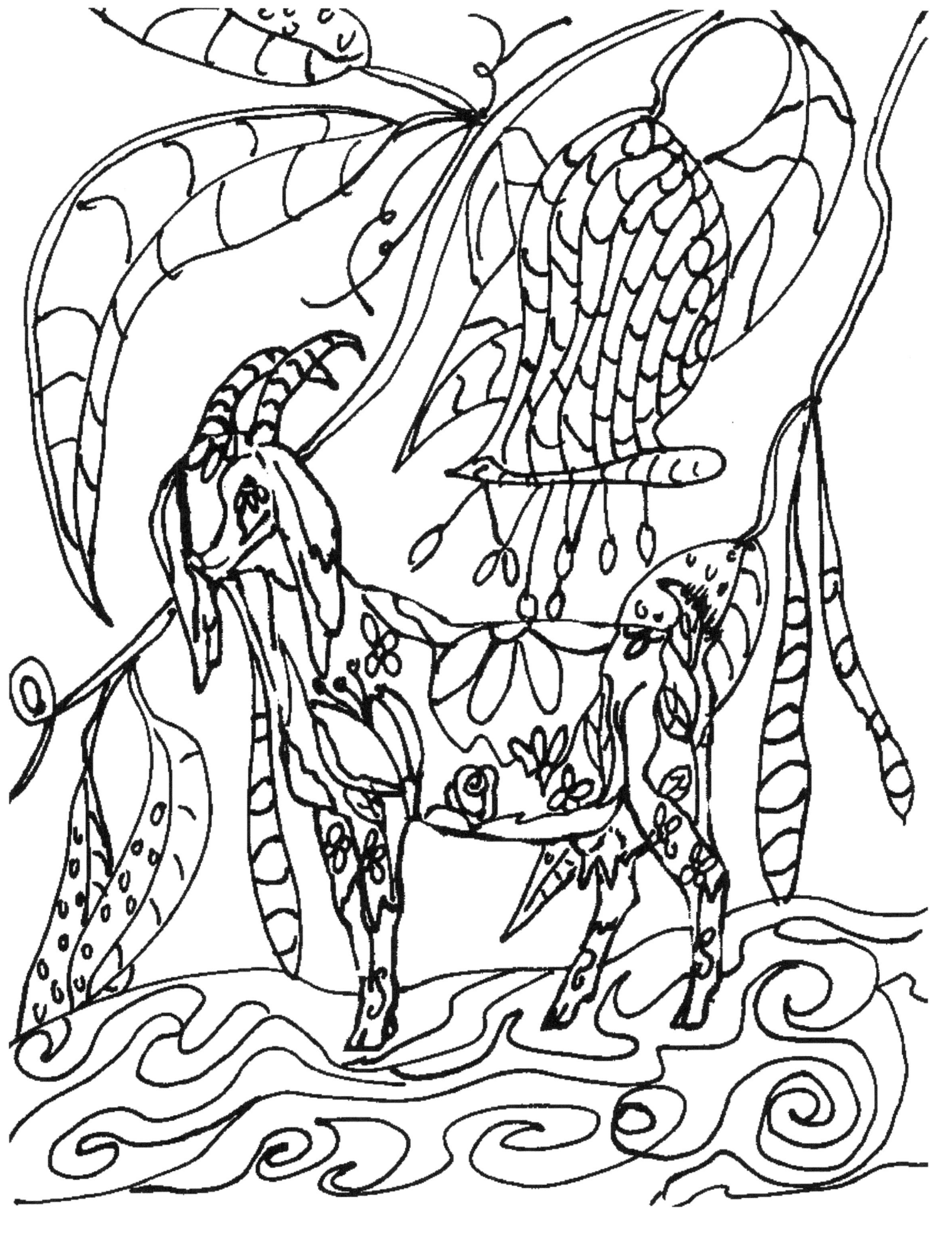

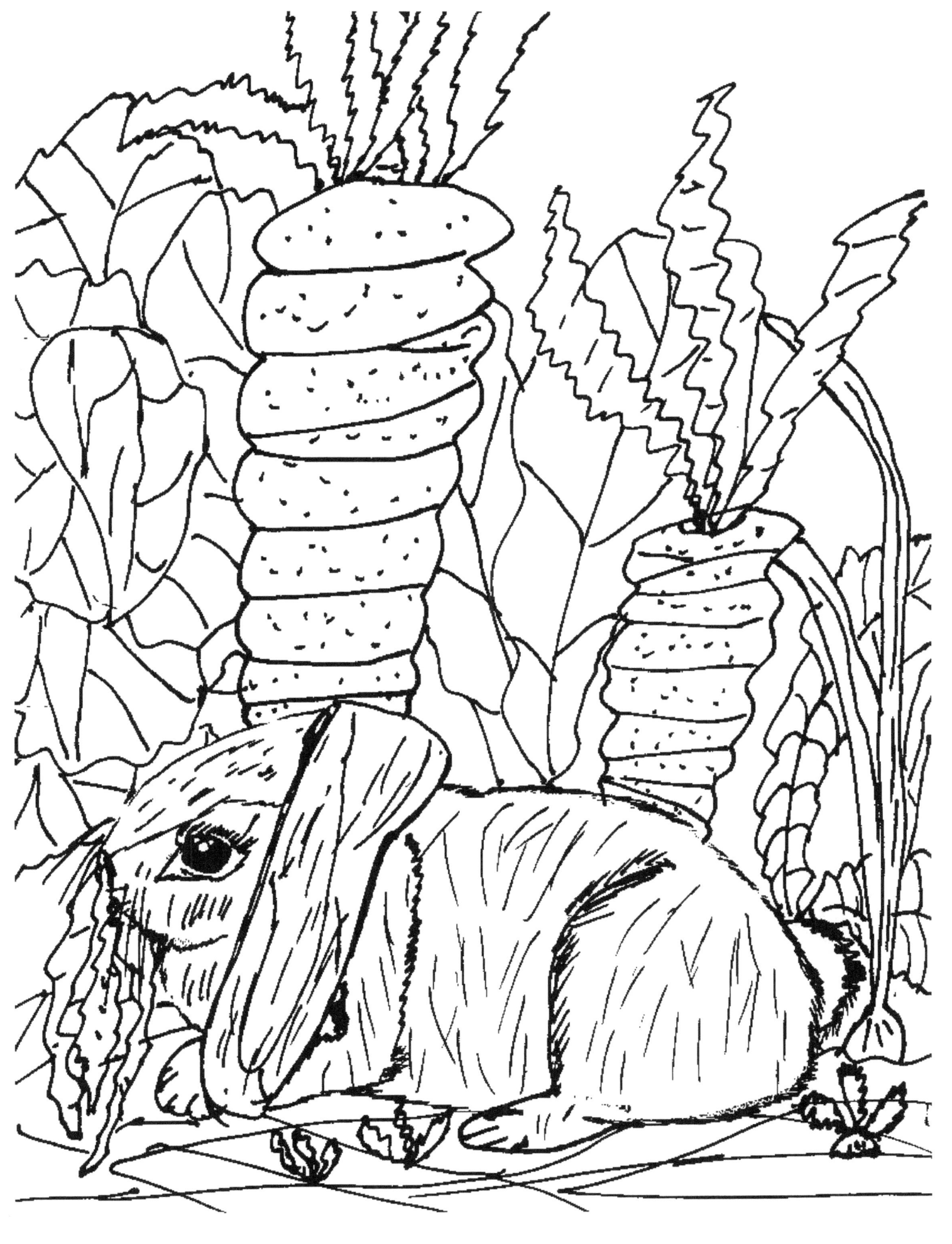

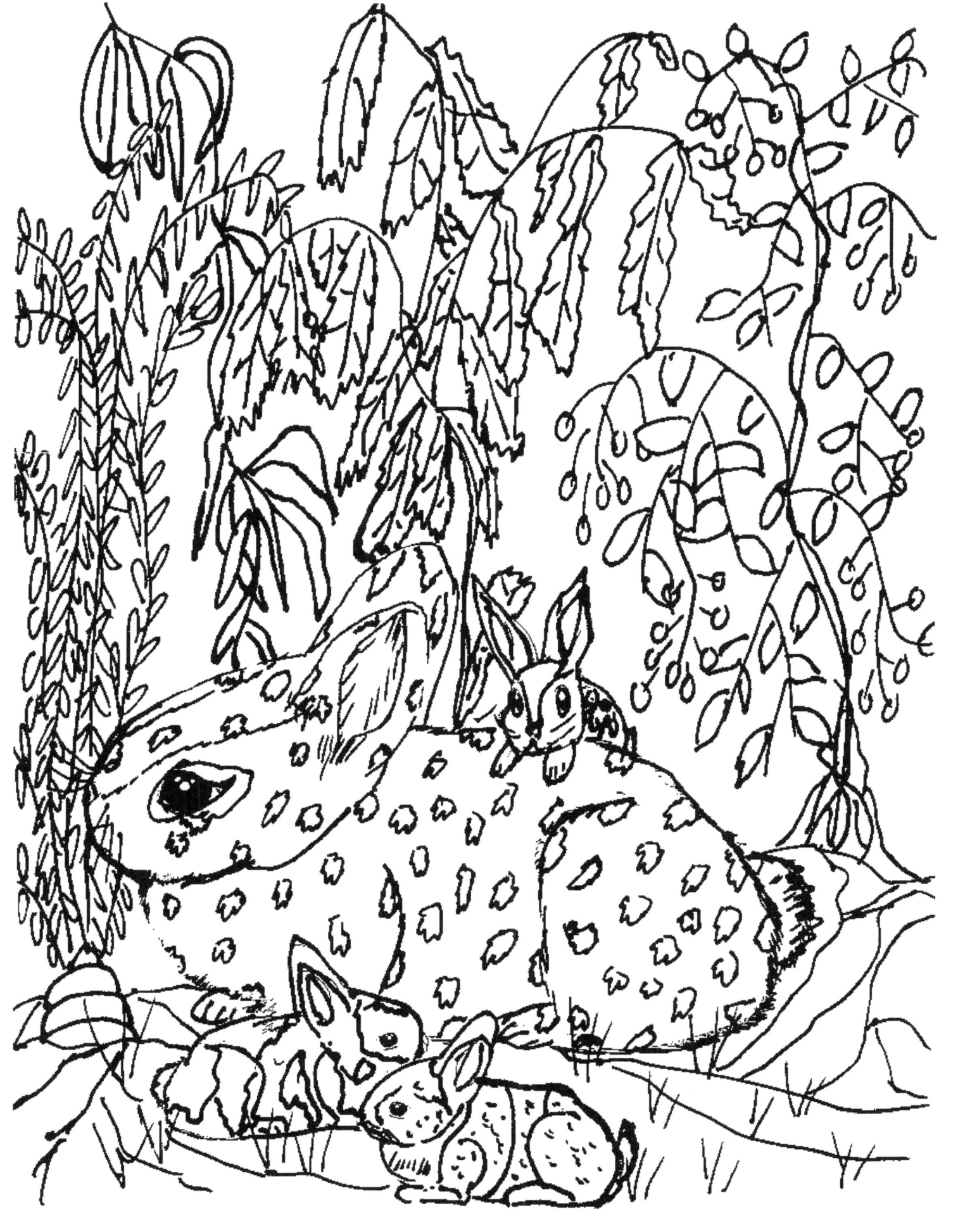

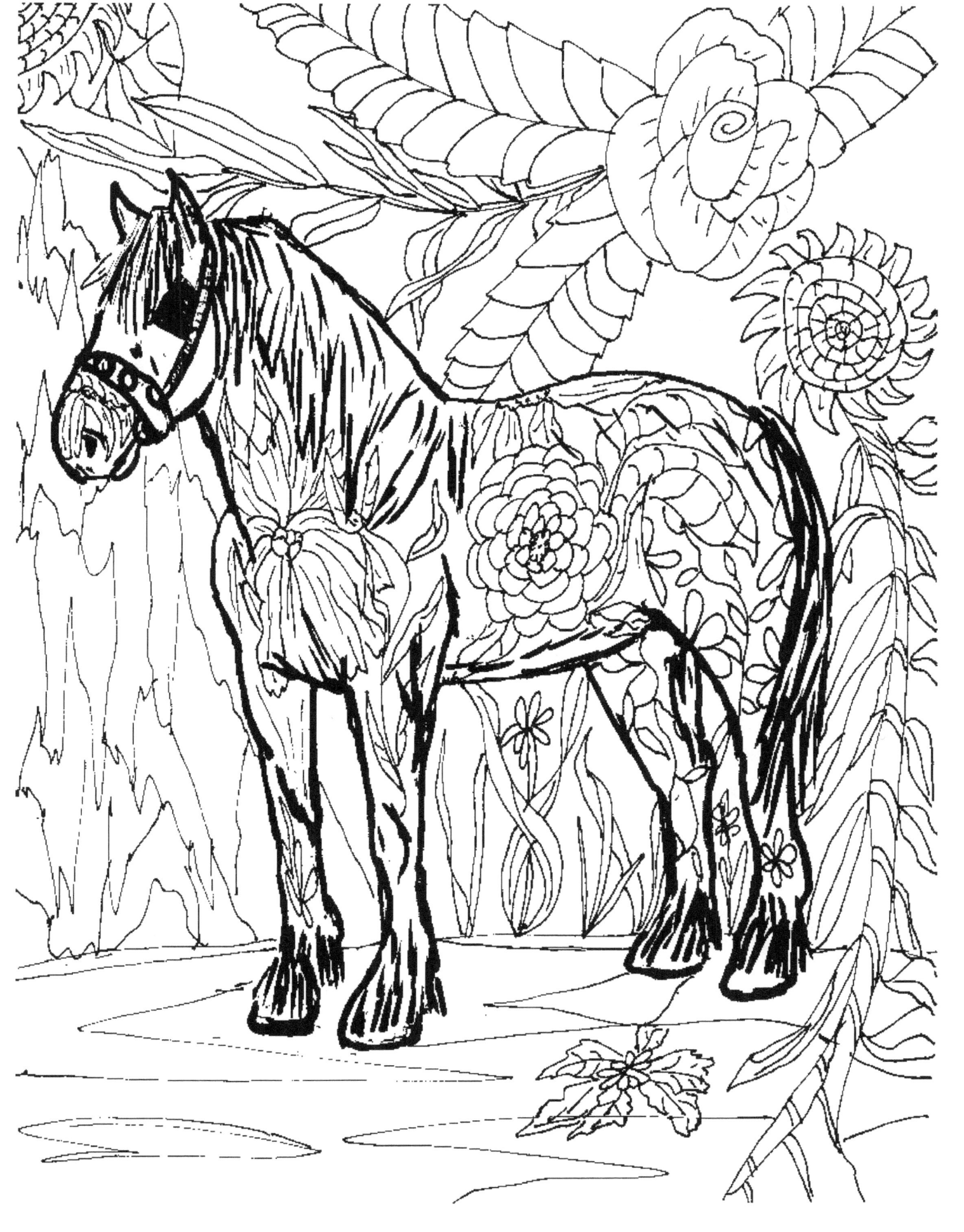

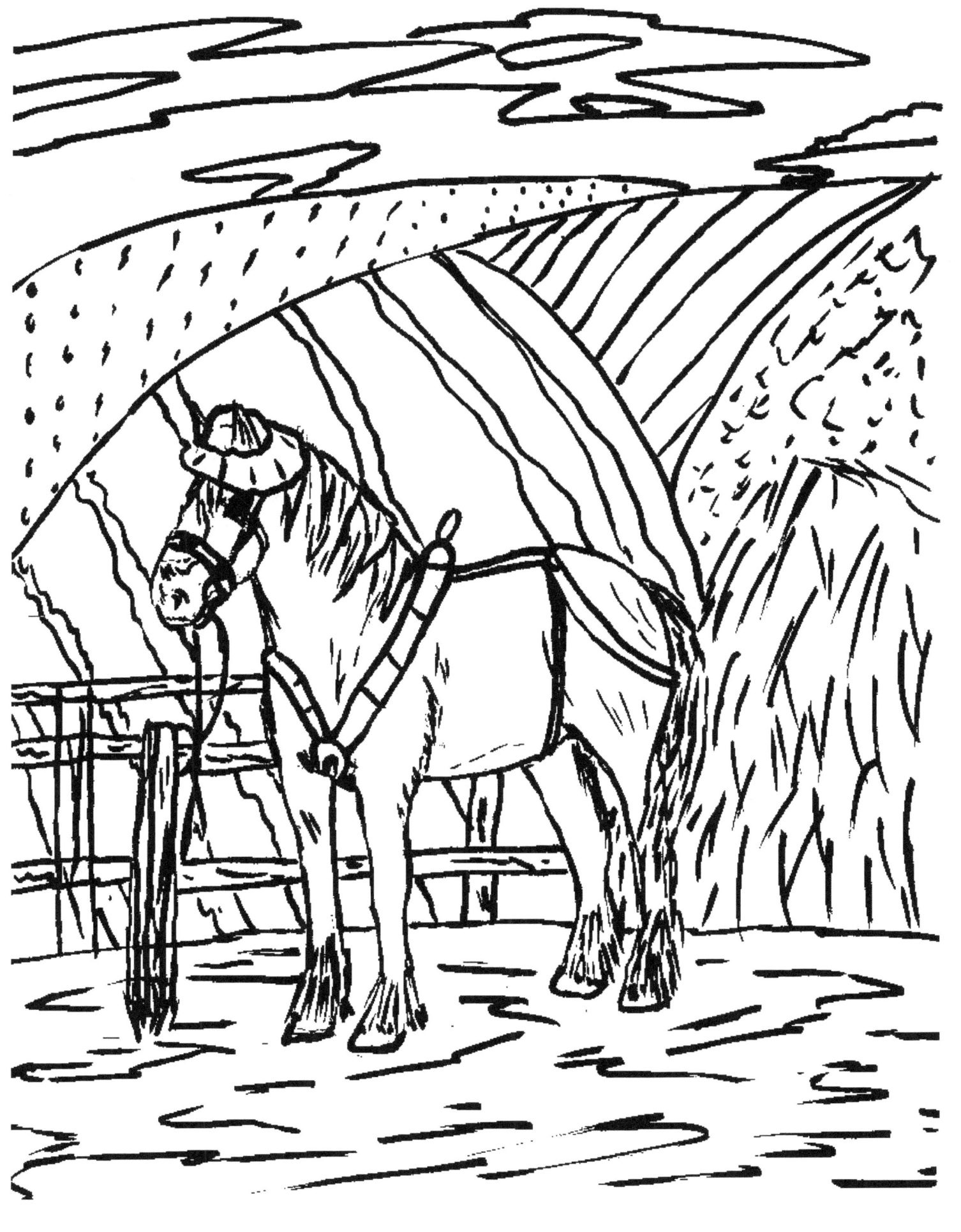

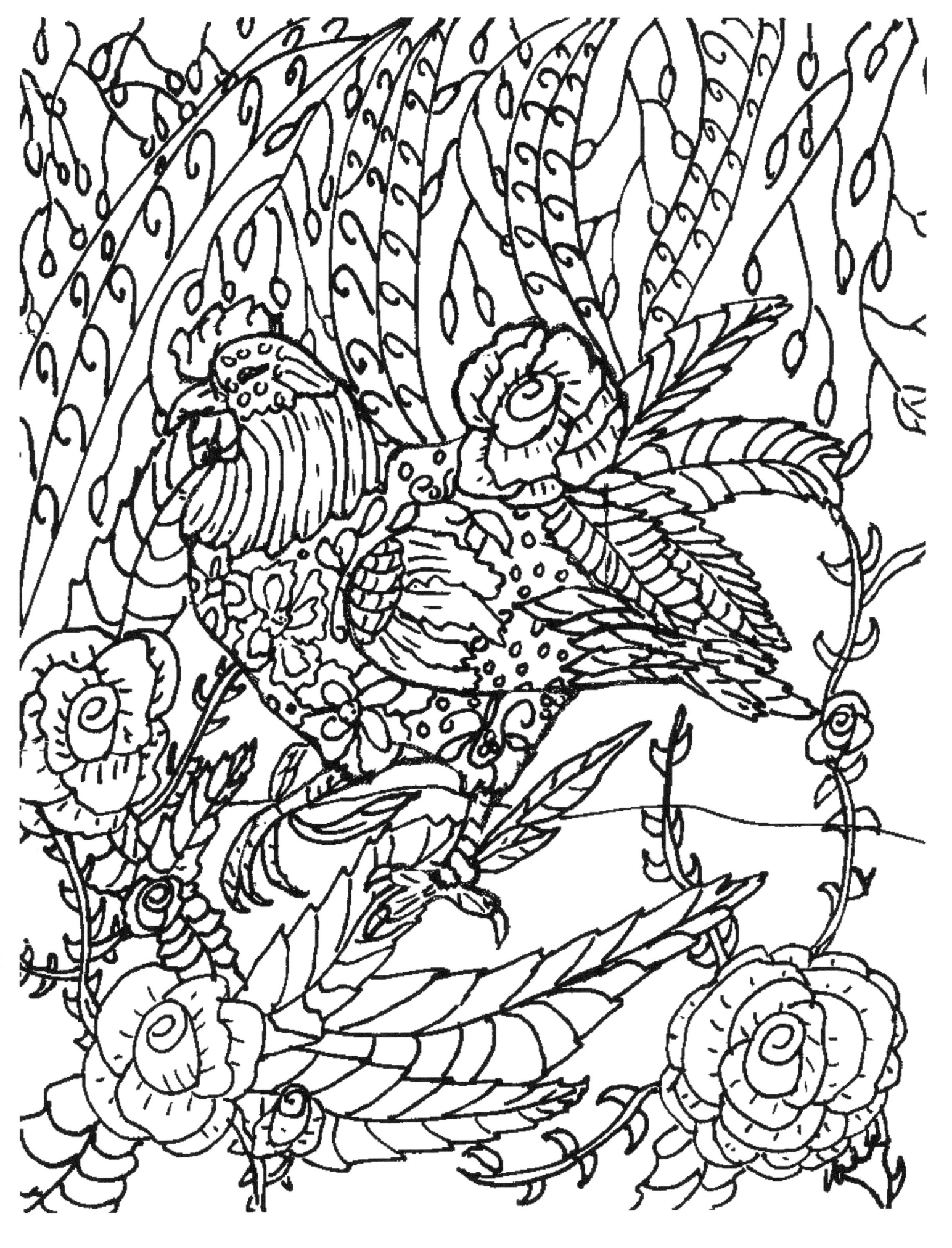

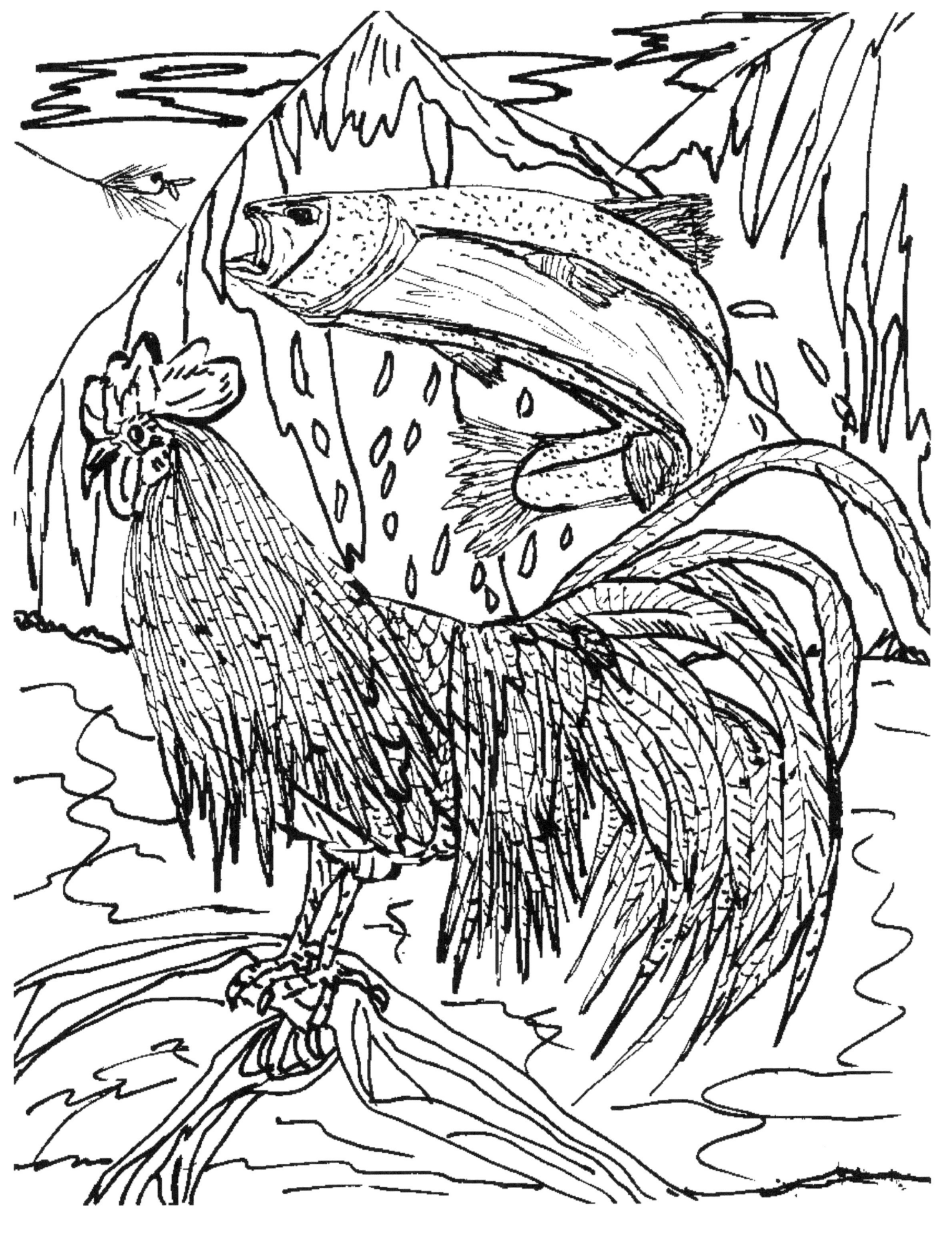

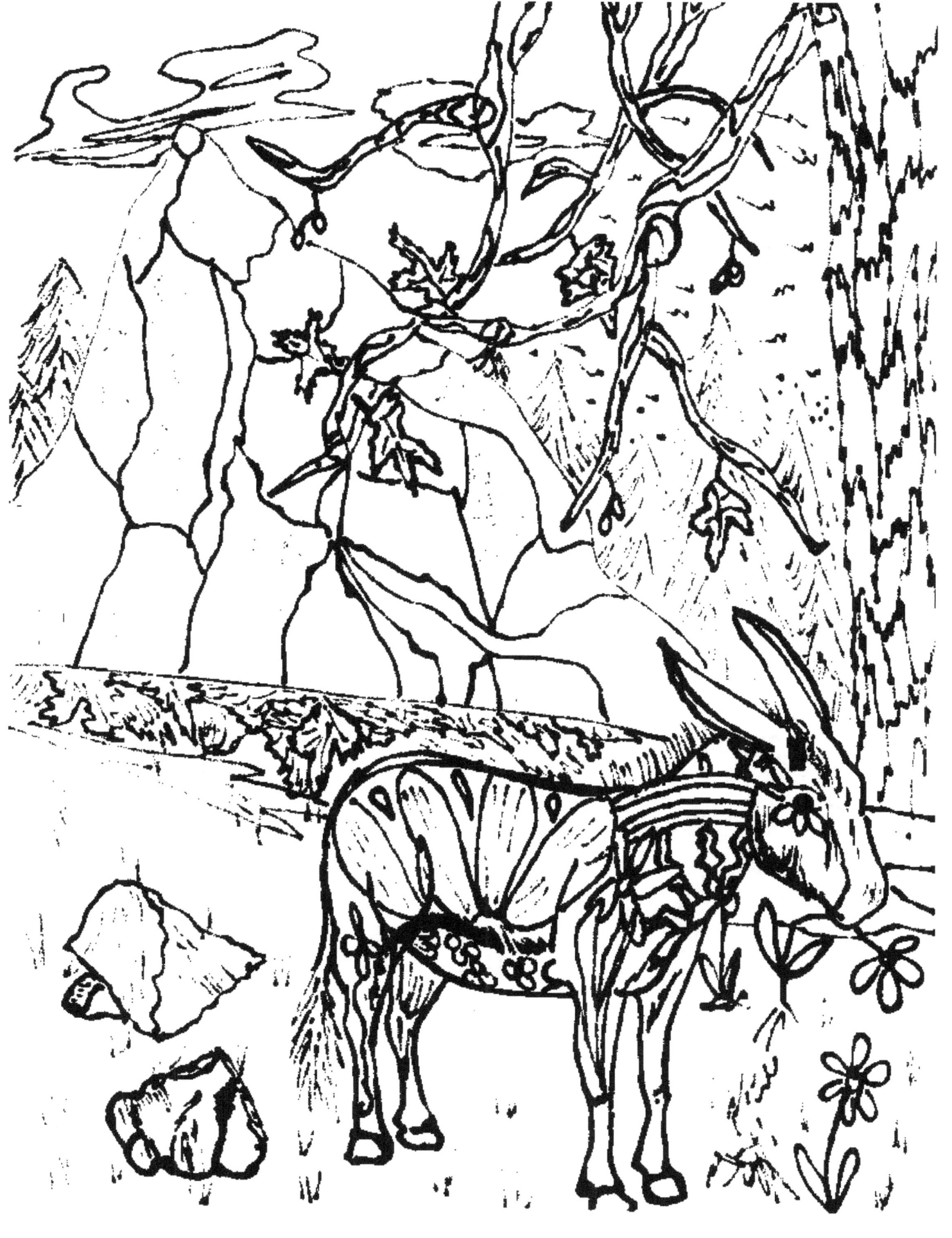

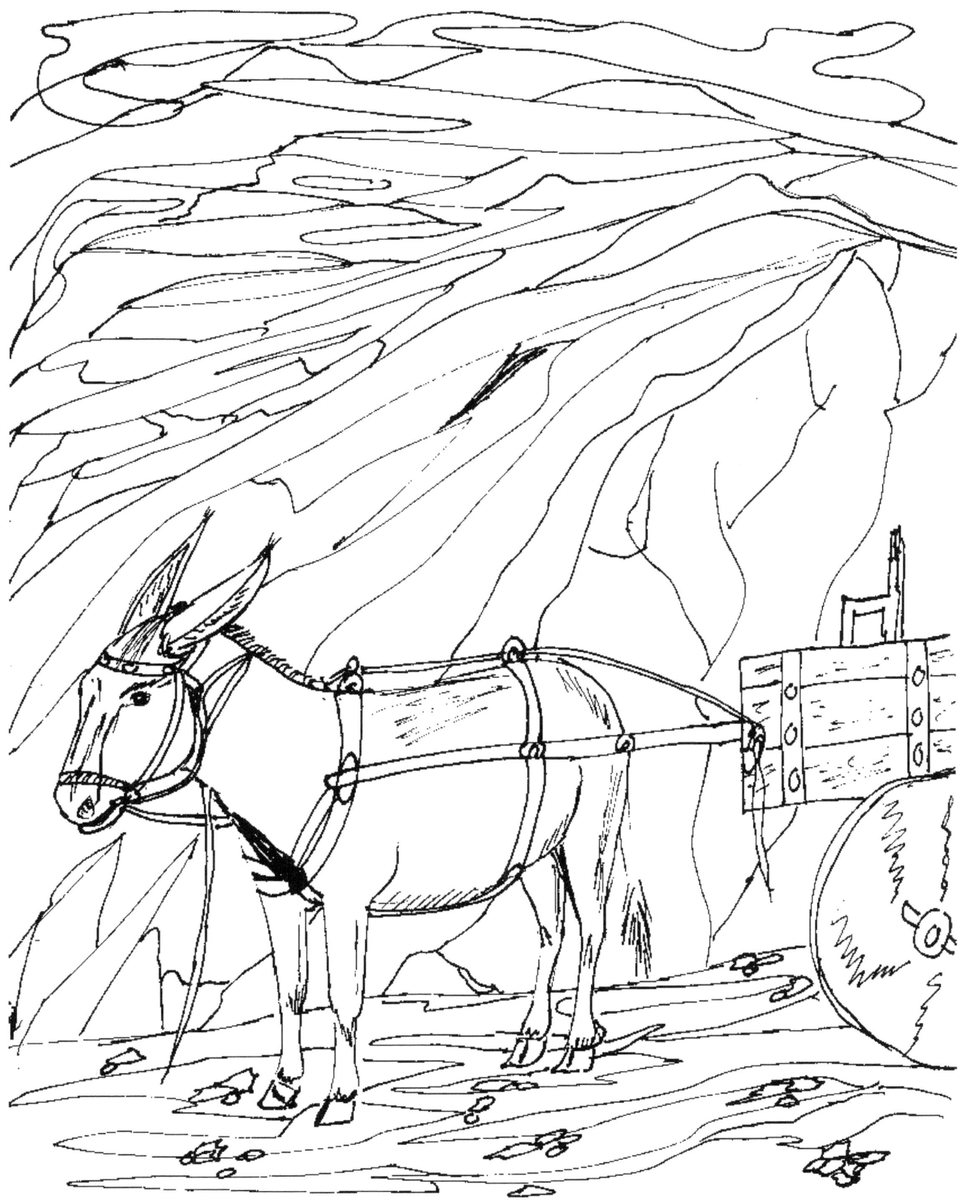

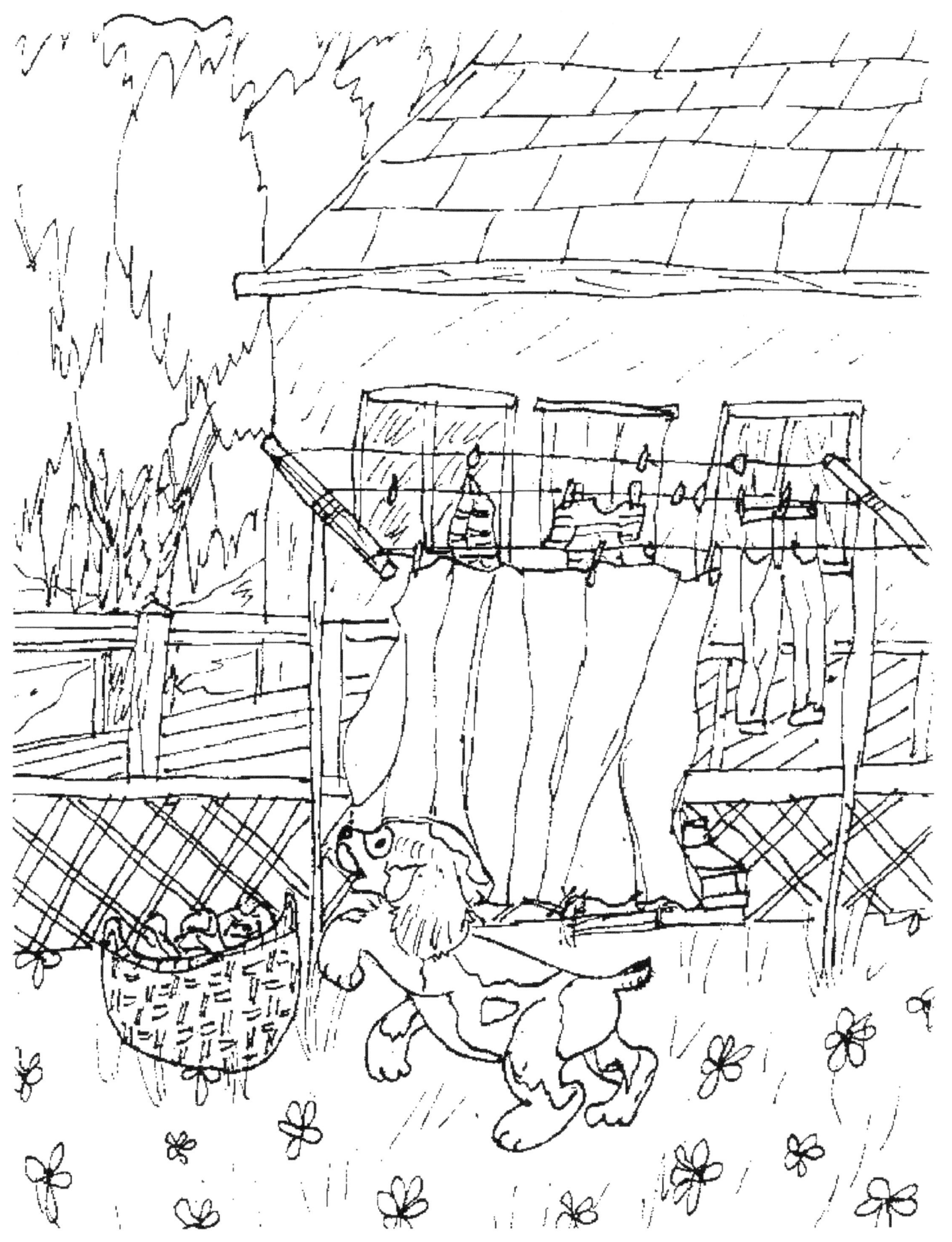

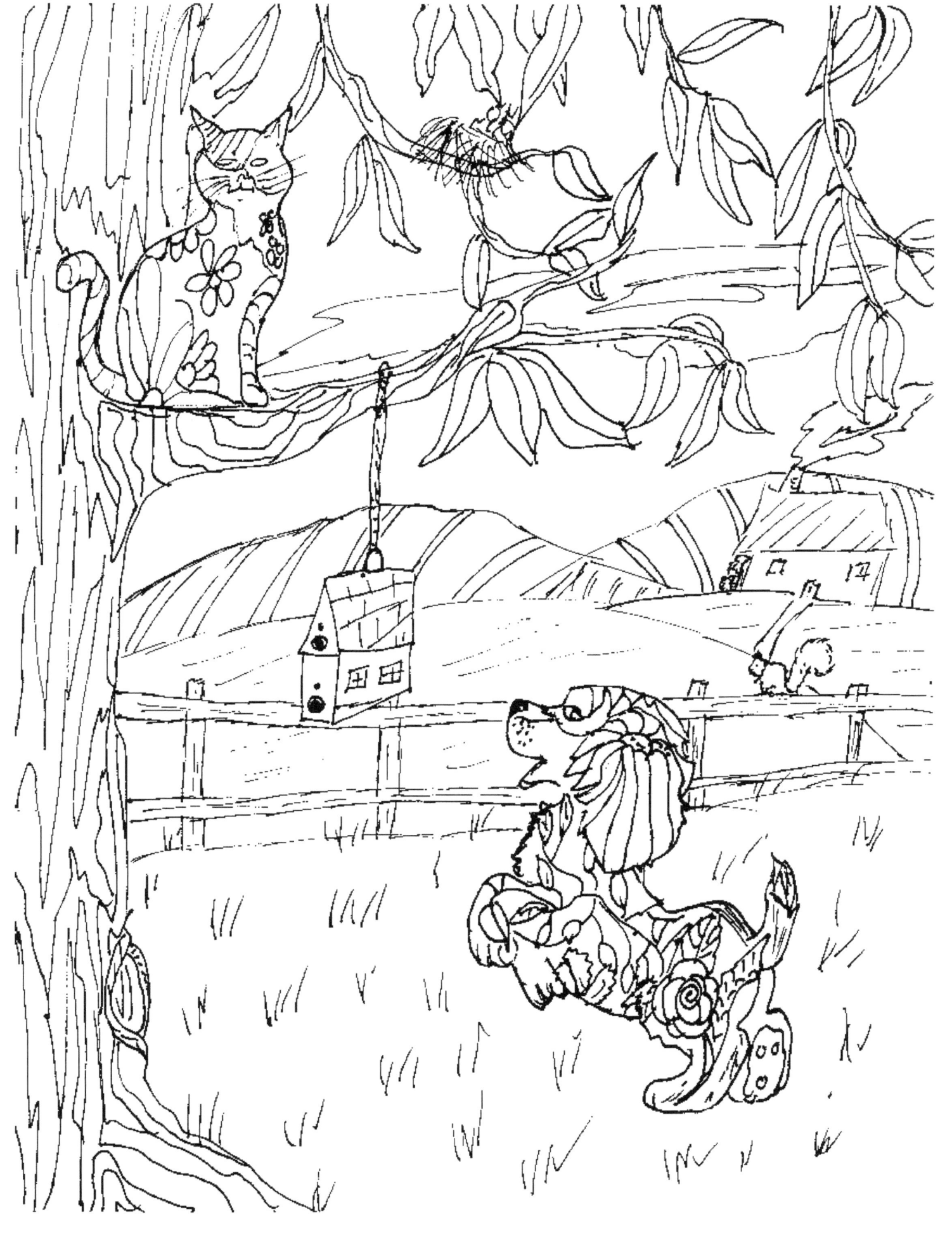